Snow
Babies

Camilla de la Bédoyère

SCHOLASTIC

This edition published by Scholastic Inc., 557 Broadway, New York, NY 10012, by arrangement with QEB Publishing, Inc.

Scholastic and associated logos are trademarks and/or registered trademarks of Scholastic Inc.

Editor: Tasha Percy
Designer: Melissa Alaverdy

Copyright © QEB Publishing, Inc. 2014

First published in the United States in 2014 by
QEB Publishing
3 Wrigley, Suite A
Irvine, CA 92618

www.qed-publishing.co.uk

A CIP record for this book is available from the Library of Congress.

ISBN 978-0-545-77087-3

10 9 8 7 6 5 4 3 2 1 0

Printed in Shenzhen City, China

Picture credits
(t=top, b=bottom, l=left, r=right)

Alamy 5tr RGB Ventures LLC dba SuperStock, 5b Patricio Robles Gil/Minden Pictures, 8 imageBROKER, 9b Philip Mugridge, 12tr Accent Alaska.com, 24tl PhotoAlto, 24b WILDLIFE GmbH, 25bl Eric Isselée, 25br GROSSEMY VANESSA, 33t Robert Harding Picture Library Ltd, 38 Robert Harding Picture Library Ltd, 39tr All Canada Photos, 39b SCPhotos, 42tl blickwinkel, 48b RGB Ventures LLC dba SuperStock, 51bl Animal Imagery, 54 AfriPics.com, 55t Purple Pilchards, 55b CRG Photo, 57tl National Geographic Image Collection, 58tl National Geographic Image Collection

Ardea 42tr Stefan Meyers

Corbis 39tl Jenny E. Ross

FLPA 2-3 Mark Raycroft/Minden Pictures, 4 Jan Vermeer/Minden Pictures, 12b Michael Quinton/Minden Pictures, 13 Donald M. Jones/Minden Pictures, 14 Jan Vermeer/Minden Pictures, 15t Frans Lanting, 15b Otto Plantema/Minden Pictures, 16l Frans Lanting, 16tr J.-L. Klein and M.-L. Hubert, 17 Fritz Polking, 18 Robert Canis, 19tl Paul Sawer, 19tr Terry Whittaker, 19b Andrew Mason, 20t Mitsuaki Iwago/Minden Pictures, 20b Jan Vermeer/Minden Pictures, 22-23 Hiroya Minakuchi/Minden Pictures, 24-25 tr Mark Raycroft/Minden Pictures, 26b Yva Momatiuk & John Eastcott/Minden Pictures, 30 Sumio Harada/Minden Pictures, 31t Sumio Harada/Minden Pictures, 31bl Jules Cox, 31br Donald M. Jones/Minden Pictures, 36 Katherine Feng/Minden Pictures, 37tl Juan-Carlos Munoz/Biosphoto, 42b Yossi Eshbol, 44 Sergey Gorshkov/Minden Pictures, 48t Donald M. Jones/Minden Pictures, 49 Michael Gore, 50b ImageBroker/Imagebroker, 50-51t Konrad Wothe/Minden Pictures, 51r F1online/ F1online, 60 Cyril Ruoso/Minden Pictures, 61tr Cyril Ruoso/Minden Pictures, 61b Xi Zhinong/Minden Pictures, 63 Yva Momatiuk & John Eastcott/Minden Pictures

Getty 1 Jan Vermeer/ Foto Natura/ Minden Pictures, 5tl Suzi Eszterhas/Minden Pictures, 9t David Courtenay Collection:Oxford Scientific, 12tl Mark Newman/Lonely Planet Images, 28-29 Darrell Gulin Collection:The Image Bank, 32 Don Johnston Collection:All Canada Photos, 33b Don Johnston Collection:All Canada Photos, 34t Norbert Rosing Collection: National Geographic, 34b Steven Kazlowski Collection:Science Faction, 35 Wayne Lynch Collection:All Canada Photos, 37tr Katherine Feng/ Globio Collection:Minden Pictures, 37b Katherine Feng/ Globio Collection:Minden Pictures, 40-41 Mark Newman Collection:Lonely Planet Images, 52-53 David & Micha Sheldon Collection:F1online, 59 Keren Su Collection:The Image Bank

NPL 6 Steven Kazlowski, 7tl Bengt Lundberg, 7tr Steven Kazlowski, 7b Steven Kazlowski, 10-11 Eric Baccega, 16br David Tipling, 21 Doug Allan, 26t Chadden Hunter, 27 Onne van der Wal, 45t Bryan and Cherry Alexander, 45b Bryan and Cherry Alexander, 46-47 Sergey Gorshkov, 56 Diane McAllister, 57tr Yukihiro Fukuda, 57b Diane McAllister, 58tr Diane McAllister, 61tl Florian Möllers, 62b Wild Wonders of Europe / Widstr

Shutterstock 43 Nataliia Melnychuk, 58b treasure dragon, 62t Lenkadan, 64 Jarry

Contents

Adélie Penguin

More than two million Adélie penguins
live in Antarctica, and its nearby islands.
Parents use stones to build their nests,
and they both take care of
the chicks.

Arctic Fox

When it is cold outside, Arctic fox
cubs stay cozy inside their burrow.
On warm days, they come out to play.
Arctic foxes grow brown coats in the
summer and white coats in the winter
to help them hide in the snow.

Brown Bear

Bear babies are very big! They are called cubs. They sleep in dens when it is very cold. Bear cubs like to roll in the snow and explore their forest home.

Snow lays thick on the ground, and there is not much food to eat in the winter. This mother bear ate plenty of berries and roots in the summer. She stored up layers of fat under her fur to keep her and her babies warm.

Dall's Sheep

It can be very cold at the top of a mountain where Dall's sheep live. Sometimes, there is still snow on the mountaintops in the summer. A mother sheep is called a ewe, and her baby is called a lamb. The lamb climbs, runs, and jumps along the rocks.

Emperor Penguin

The Antarctic is the coldest place on Earth. Winter lasts for six months. Life is hard, but millions of penguins make their homes there. Emperor penguin babies are called chicks. They hatch out of their eggs in the middle of winter.

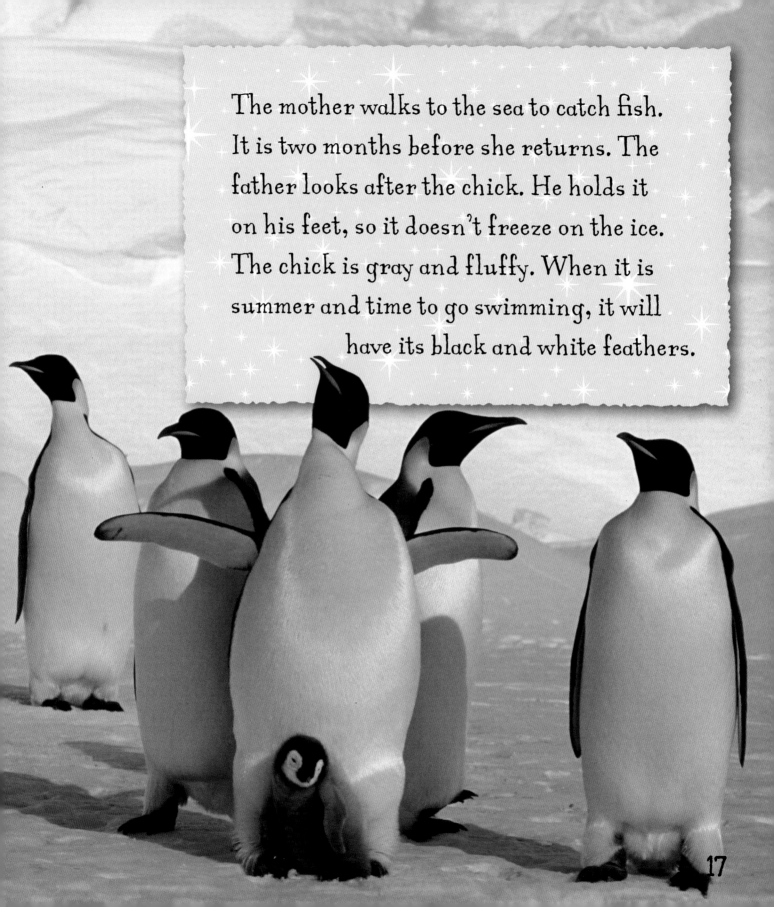

The mother walks to the sea to catch fish. It is two months before she returns. The father looks after the chick. He holds it on his feet, so it doesn't freeze on the ice. The chick is gray and fluffy. When it is summer and time to go swimming, it will have its black and white feathers.

17

Fallow Deer

Little fallow deer fawns are always looking and listening for danger. They move quickly when they are scared. Fawns have brown fur with white spots. When the spring comes, they will hide under bushes or trees.

Harp Seal

Harp seals spend most of their time swimming in the icy Arctic Ocean. They have thick layers of fat and fur to keep them warm. Baby seals are called pups. They have white fur.

A pup cannot swim until it has grown a new coat of dark fur. It gets very hungry while it waits for the new fur to grow. This pup is waiting for its mother to dive into the water and find some crabs and fish to eat.

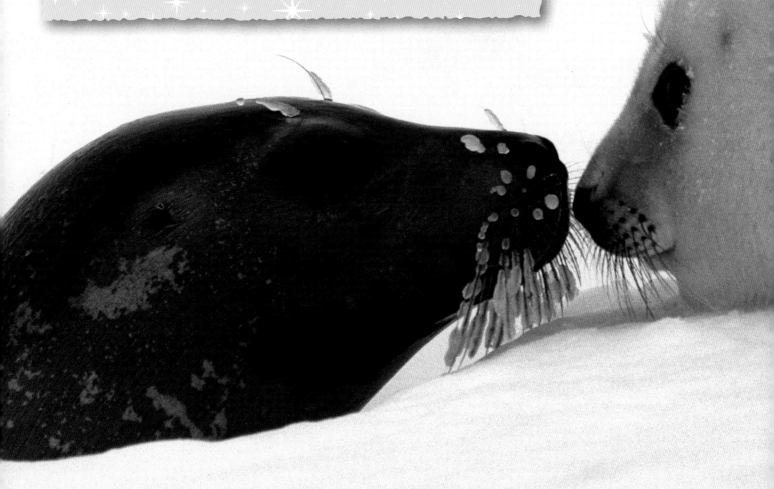

23

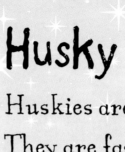

Husky

Huskies are clever and friendly animals. They are fast runners, and they love to chase each other in the snow. Huskies are Arctic dogs that live where the winters are very long and ice-cold winds blow. They live in groups, called packs, and huddle together to keep warm.

King Penguin

King penguins lay their eggs in the spring and look after their chicks in the summer, when it is still cold and snowy! These water-loving birds live near the South Pole.

26

King penguin chicks don't look like their mom or dad. They have round, brown fluffy bodies and are sometimes called "woolly penguins." While their parents hunt for fish, the chicks huddle together to stay warm.

29

Mountain Goat

Mountain goats climb up hills and cliffs to hide from bears, wolves, and mountain lions. Even baby goats, known as kids, can skip through the snow without slipping. Mountain goats eat plants and nibble on snow when they are thirsty.

Mountain Lion

The snow is deep, but a cute mountain lion cub doesn't mind! Cubs start to play when they are ten days old. They practice pouncing, chasing, and hiding. Mountain lions are also called pumas.

Muskox

Muskox families spend the whole year in the Arctic, even during the freezing winter months when there is little grass to eat. The adults take good care of their calves and protect them from wolves and bears.

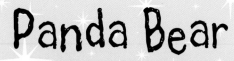

Panda Bear

A panda bear cub is so tiny when it is born that it weighs the same as an apple. Soon, it is big enough to play outside in the snow. Giant pandas climb trees and eat bamboo.

Polar Bear

Little cubs keep an eye open for danger. When they are bigger, they will be fearless. Polar bears live in the Arctic, and they love the snow. Their fur is so thick that they can get too hot in the summer!

Polar bears are the world's biggest bears. Mom builds her cubs a den, so they are born in a warm, safe place. In the spring, the fluffy cubs come out of the den to explore and learn how to hunt.

Red Fox

Little red fox cubs are often born before the spring sunshine comes. Their mother keeps them snug inside her den while they grow strong. Soon, they can leave their home to play outside. If they get too chilly or wet, they go back inside to warm up.

Reindeer

Little reindeer calves graze on grass just one hour after being born. When they are a day old, they can run faster than a person. Reindeer are also called caribou. They are able to smell grass under a layer of deep snow!

44

The snow is melting and a calf must eat a lot to grow big and strong. At the end of the summer, it will join its herd on a long journey south to keep out of the worst of the winter weather.

Sea Otter

These pups love to cuddle! They are sea otter babies and will stay close to their mom. Sometimes sea otters hold hands. The water is chilly, but sea otters have the thickest fur of any animal in the world.

Siberian Tiger

Tigers hunt at night, but in the deep winter they often hunt in the day, too. Little cubs love to play fight, which is a good way to become a great hunter.

50

Mother tigers usually have up to six cubs at a time. The cubs are born blind and helpless. They need their mom to look after them until they are three years old. She will fight other animals to protect them.

Snow Leopard

Very few people have ever seen a snow leopard, and cubs are especially shy. These wild cats live on wintry, windy mountains in Asia. Sleeping snow leopards wrap their tails around themselves like a blanket.

Snow Monkey
(Japanese Macaque)

Snow monkeys like the snow. It's a chilly day, but the water is nice and warm! There is deep snow lying around, but a baby snow monkey can jump into the hot springs to warm up.

The babies even make snowballs just for fun. While the youngsters play, moms and dads soak in the water to keep warm. Snow monkeys are also called Japanese macaques.

Snub-Nosed Monkey

The winters are long and harsh where snub-nosed monkeys live. Little babies don't mind. They have lots of fur to keep them warm. They also get snuggly cuddles from their mom, granny, and aunts!

Wild Pony

Ponies are small horses. They live on grasslands where they spend the day grazing on plants with the rest of the herd. Baby ponies are called foals and stay close to mom.

Horses and ponies grow fur and a long mane to keep them dry, even in rain and snow. When they get chilly, ponies gallop around to warm themselves up again!

64